GETTING BY IN FRENCH

A quick beginners' course for tourists and businesspeople

Course writer: Celia Weber
Producer: Christopher Stone
Executive Producer: Edith Baer

D1040995

BARRON'S/Woodbury, New York/London/Toronto
By arrangement with the British Broadcasting Corporation

First U.S. Edition published in 1982 by Barron's Educational Series, Inc.

By arrangement with the British Broadcasting Corporation, 35 Marylebone High Street, London W1M 4AA.

English version © The British Broadcasting Corporation and the 1978 Contributors.

All rights reserved.
No part of this book may be reproduced in any form, by photostat, microfilm, xerography, or any other means, or incorporated into any information retrieval system, electronic or mechanical, without the written permission of the copyright owner.

All inquiries should be addressed to:
Barron's Educational Series, Inc.
113 Crossways Park Drive
Woodbury, New York 11797

International Standard Book No. 0-8120-2574-1

PRINTED IN THE UNITED STATES OF AMERICA

2345   047   98765432

Contents

The course . . . and how to use it   4

Programme 1   **Getting to meet people**   6
Saying hello   7
Saying how you are   7
Ordering a drink of beer; tea;
coffee   8

Programme 2   **Getting somewhere to stay**   15
Booking a hotel room   15
Checking in   16
Ordering breakfast   16

Programme 3   **Getting your shopping done**   24
Buying eggs; milk; wine; fruit;
butter; bread; petrol; stamps; an
English newspaper   24

Programme 4   **Getting around**   34
Looking for a car park; the Post
Office; the town centre; the Place de
la Mairie; a restaurant; the Syndicat
d'Initiative; the Palais de Justice;
the station   34
Buying a ticket   36

Test your skill   Exercises to check during
programme 5   **44**

Programme 5   **Getting a meal out**   46
Asking for the menu or a set
meal   46
Choosing an aperitif   46
Saying how you'd like your
meat   46
Ordering vegetables   47
Choosing a dessert   47

Reference section
Extra language notes   53
Pronunciation guide   53
Numbers   56
Days of the week   57
Months of the year   57
Useful addresses   58
Key to exercises   58
French–English word list   60
English–French word list   65

The course...and how to use it

Getting by in French is a
five-programme radio
course for anyone
planning a visit to a
French-speaking
country. It provides, in a
short learning period, a
basic 'survival kit' for
some of the situations
typical of a visit abroad.

'Getting by' means

- managing to keep your head above water
- having a go at making yourself understood
- listening for clues so that you can get the gist of what's said
- knowing how to look up what you don't understand
- knowing how to take short cuts
- getting more fun out of your trip abroad

Each programme

- concentrates on the language you'll need to say and understand to cope with a particular situation — getting something to eat and drink, booking a room in a hotel, asking the way . . .
- includes real-life conversations, specially recorded in France, to let you hear everyday French right from the start
- gives you opportunities to repeat new words and expressions aloud in the pauses and to work out for yourself how to 'get by' before you hear the answers

The book includes

- the texts of the conversations heard in the programmes
- a summary of what you'll need to say, and listen out for
- brief language notes
- tips about everyday life in France
- self-checking exercises for you to do between programmes

At the end of the book, there are some extra language notes, a pronunciation guide, a section on numbers, days of the week and months of the year, a list of useful addresses, the answers to the exercises and a word list.

To make the most of the course

During the programmes take every opportunity of repeating aloud what you are asked to say, and concentrate on listening out for clues. With the cassettes you may prefer to go through each programme in sections. The pauses for your reply are timed to allow for a little thought but a fairly prompt answer. If the pauses seem too short at first, lengthen them by stopping the machine.
After the programmes read the conversations aloud, with someone else if possible. If you have the cassettes, check your pronunciation by imitating the speakers phrase by phrase, using the pause button to stop the tape. Then read through the book chapter and do the exercises, looking up any words and phrases you don't know in the word list.
Before listening to the next programme read through the next chapter in advance.

When you go abroad take this book with you, plus a good pocket dictionary and a notebook, so you can jot down the things you discover for yourself. If you can *Get by in French* you'll enjoy your visit all the more! *Bonne chance!*

1 Getting to meet people

Conversations

These conversations are included in the programme.
Read them aloud, with someone else if possible, as
often as you can after you have listened to the
broadcasts or cassettes. If you have the cassettes
use them to check your pronunciation. Look up any
words and phrases you don't know in the word list
on page 60.

Before attempting the conversations you may prefer
to go through the Explanations section that follows.

The underlined parts are the absolute minimum
you need to say to 'get by'.

Changing traveller's cheques at the bank

Cliente	Bonjour madame.
Employée	Bonjour madame.
Cliente	Je voudrais changer de l'argent, s'il vous plaît.
Employée	Oui, quelle monnaie?
Cliente	En travellers.
Employée	Vous avez un passeport?
Cliente	Oui, bien sûr. Voilà.

Employée	Merci. Voilà, vous signez là, s'il vous plaît, vos traveller's checks.
Cliente	Bien, merci.

je voudrais changer de l'argent   *I'd like to change some money*

No room at the hotel

Réceptionniste Oui monsieur, mais j'ai le regret de vous dire nous sommes complet.

j'ai le regret de vous dire nous sommes complet   *I'm sorry, we're fully booked*

Saying good morning, good afternoon

Mme Cabillic <u>Bonjour mademoiselle.</u> Je suis Madame Cabillic. Je voudrais parler à Monsieur Dujardin, s'il vous plaît. Allô! <u>Bonjour monsieur</u>!

allô – *only used on the phone to find out if someone's there*

. . . good evening

Une femme	<u>Bonsoir monsieur.</u>
Un homme	<u>Bonsoir madame.</u>

. . . and goodbye

Une femme	<u>Au revoir monsieur.</u>
Un homme	<u>Au revoir madame.</u>

Saying how you are

Mme Launay	Bonjour Madame Cabillic.
Mme Cabillic	<u>Bonjour Madame Launay.</u>
Mme Launay	Comment allez-vous?
Mme Cabillic	<u>Très bien, merci.</u>

. . . and in a more friendly way

Mme Launay	Bonjour Madame Cabillic.
Mme Cabillic	<u>Bonjour Madame Launay.</u>
Mme Launay	Ça va?
Mme Cabillic	<u>Ça va, merci.</u>

Asking for a beer

Client	S'il vous plait!
Serveuse	Oui monsieur?
Client	Une bière, s'il vous plaît.
Serveuse	Oui monsieur, une bière. Vous désirez une bière – bouteille ou une bière pression?
Client	Une pression.

bouteille ou une bière pression?   *a bottle – or draught beer?*

. . . a cup of tea

Serveuse	Vous désirez un café, un thé?
Cliente	Un thé.
Serveuse	Un thé citron, un thé nature, un thé au lait?
Cliente	Un thé au lait.

. . . or coffee

Client	Un café noir, s'il vous plaît.
Serveuse	Un café noir. Oui monsieur.

What you'll need to say during the programme . . .

Hello and goodbye

bonjour		madame
bonsoir	*to be polite add:*	mademoiselle
au revoir		monsieur

Attracting someone's attention
s'il vous plaît!

Saying how you are
très bien, merci – *or, more friendly* – ça va, merci

Asking for something to drink

une bière	‖ *choose from:*	une bouteille
		une pression

un thé	citron nature au lait	un café	noir crème

Numbers

0	1	2	3	4	5
zéro	un	deux	trois	quatre	cinq

6	7	8	9	10
six	sept	huit	neuf	dix

. . . and to listen out for

How are you?
comment allez-vous? – *or, more friendly* – ça va?

What would you like?
vous désirez? *or*
que désirez-vous?

Explanations

Masculine and feminine words
In French, both people *and* things are either
masculine or feminine.

a coffee is *un* café   *the* coffee is *le* café
          but   but
a beer is *une* bière   *the* beer is *la* bière

un/le in front of a word shows it's masculine
(marked *m* in dictionaries).
une/la in front of a word shows it's feminine
(marked *f* in dictionaries).

When you learn a new word, remember it with
un/le or *une/la* in front of it.

Le and *la* are shortened to *l'* in front of all words
beginning with a vowel and most words beginning
with 'h' in order to make a smoother sound.
(In French 'h' is never sounded.)
  e.g. *le* sandwich   but   *l'*hôtel and *l'*apértif

Worth knowing

Saying hello and goodbye

bonjour hello to anyone, at any time of day, until evening: then it's *bonsoir*.

au revoir goodbye anytime. Shake hands with colleagues and friends each time you meet, and when you say goodbye.

allô only used to find out if someone's at the other end of the telephone.

Saying please and thank you

s'il vous plaît please, when you want something, or to attract someone's attention

merci thank you for something you've been given, or
in reply to something being offered, means no thank you

How to address people

monsieur to a man
madame to a married or older woman
mademoiselle to a young woman or girl

Of course if you know them use their name! e.g. *Bonjour Madame Launay*.

It's polite to add *monsieur, madame* or *mademoiselle* when saying *bonjour* – *bonsoir* – *au revoir* – *merci* – *s'il vous plaît*.

Where to get light refreshments

bar the place for a quick drink.

café depending on size a *café* may serve hot drinks, alcoholic and soft drinks, ice-cream, snacks and sandwiches: things are more expensive if you sit outside on the *terrasse*. *Cafés* are often open from early morning until late evening. If you see the TABAC sign displayed (see page 29) you can also get cigarettes and stamps.

café brasserie	similar to a café but also serves meals.
buffet	for a quick meal at the counter or a table. They often stay open very late.
self	a self-service snack bar.
salon de thé	elegant and expensive. You can get tea, coffee and cakes and pastries.
friterie	a chip stall. The place to buy packets of chips often served with mayonnaise, especially in Belgium.
crêperie	for sweet and savoury pancakes *(crêpes)*: they are most common in Brittany and Normandy. There are also waffles *(gauffrettes)*.

Some popular drinks and snacks

beer	*une bière*	a bottle *une bouteille* draught *une pression*
cider	*un cidre*	
coffee	*un café*	black *noir* white *crème*
fruit juice	*un jus de fruit*	
orange juice	*un jus d'orange*	
tomato juice	*un jus de tomate*	
lemonade	*une limonade*	
orangeade	*une orangeade*	
tea *un thé*		lemon *citron* with milk *au lait* nothing added *nature*
a glass of water	*un verre d'eau*	
hot dog	*un hot dog*	
omelette	*une omelette*	
pancake	*une crêpe*	
sandwich	*un sandwich*	
cheese sandwich	*un sandwich au fromage*	
ham sandwich	*un sandwich au jambon*	
pâté sandwich	*un sandwich au pâté*	
salami sandwich	*un sandwich au saucisson*	
toasted sandwich	(open with ham and cheese) *un croque-monsieur*.	

Exercises

1 Complete the captions, choosing the most suitable from the following:

au revoir mademoiselle / ça va merci / une bière / et un sandwich au jambon / s'il vous plaît ! / et un croque-monsieur / merci madame / merci mademoiselle / au revoir madame / bonjour madame

2 How do you say 'hello', 'goodbye' and 'thank you' to the people below? Fill in the captions and then practise saying them out loud.

a	b

c	d

3 You are the only one who knows any French. Order drinks and snacks for everyone. Sort out what everyone wants then write the whole order out in French.

4 Complete the captions below:

a_ _ _ _ _ _ _ _

b_ _ _ _ _ _ _ _ _

c_ _ _ _ _ _ _ _ _

d_ _ _ _ _ _ _ _

e_ _ _ _ _ _ _ _ _ _

f_ _ _ _ _ _ _ _ _ _

5 Practise saying these numbers:

8	7	5	4	0
huit	sept	cinq	quatre	zéro

9	3	1	6
neuf	trois	un	six

2 Getting somewhere to stay

Conversations

Booking a hotel room

Client	<u>Bonjour madame.</u>
Réceptionniste	Bonjour monsieur.
Client	Vous avez <u>une chambre</u> pour ce soir?
Réceptionniste	Oui, pour combien de personnes monsieur?
Client	Pour <u>deux personnes.</u>
Réceptionniste	Vous désirez un grand lit, ou deux lits?
Client	<u>Deux lits, s'il vous plaît.</u>
Réceptionniste	Avec bain ou cabinet de toilette monsieur?
Client	<u>Avec cabinet de toilette</u>.
Réceptionniste	Oui, c'est pour combien de nuits, monsieur?
Client	Pour <u>trois nuits.</u>
Réceptionniste	Bien, nous avons une chambre au deuxième étage. C'est la chambre numéro vingt et un.
Client	Le numéro vingt et un?
Réceptionniste	Oui, monsieur.
Client	Et c'est <u>combien</u>?
Réceptionniste	Le prix de la chambre est de cent francs, prix net, taxes et service compris.

vous avez une chambre pour ce soir?   *do you have a room for tonight?*

prix net, taxes et service compris   *net price, tax and service included*

Booking a room with a shower

Réceptionniste	Vous voulez une chambre avec un cabinet de toilette ou une douche?
Client	<u>Avec une douche</u> de préférence.
Réceptionniste	Avec une douche.

de préférence *preferably*

Checking in

M. Launay	<u>Bonjour madame. J'ai réservé une chambre.</u>
Réceptionniste	Oui, bonjour monsieur, c'est à quel nom?
M. Launay	Au nom de <u>Monsieur Launay</u>.
Réceptionniste	Oui, c'est une chambre pour une personne ou pour deux personnes?
M. Launay	Pour <u>deux personnes</u>.
Réceptionniste	Bien, entendu! Votre chambre c'est le numéro soixante et un. C'est au troisième étage.
M. Launay	Le numéro soixante et un au troisième étage.

c'est à quel nom? *what name is it?*
au nom de M. Launay *my name is Mr Launay*
bien, entendu! *right!*

Ordering breakfast

Serveuse	Bonjour monsieur.
Client	<u>Bonjour madame. Un petit déjeuner, s'il vous plaît.</u>
Serveuse	Oui monsieur, qu'est-ce que vous allez prendre? Café noir, café au lait, thé citron, thé au lait, ou chocolat?
Client	Bien, je vais prendre <u>un chocolat</u>, s'il vous plaît.
Serveuse	Un chocolat. Avec pain ou avec croissants?
Client	<u>Avec</u> des <u>croissants</u>.
Serveuse	Avec des croissants.

Client	Merci.
Serveuse	Très bien, monsieur, merci.

qu'est-ce que vous allez prendre? *what are you going to have?*
je vais prendre *I'll have*
avec des croissants *or* avec croissants *with croissants*

What you'll need to say during the programme . . .

A room please
une chambre s'il vous plaît.

I've booked a room
j'ai réservé une chambre.

For 1, 2, 3 . . . nights/people

une, deux, trois . . . nuit(s)
personne(s)

A double bed or two singles
un grand lit   deux lits

What toilet facilities

avec | bain
cabinet de toilette
une douche

How much is it?
combien?

Ordering breakfast
un petit déjeuner, s'il vous plaît.

un café	noir au lait		
			pain
un thé	citron au lait nature	avec	
			croissants
un chocolat			

If you don't understand what people say

pardon | monsieur?
| madame?
| mademoiselle?

If you want them to speak more slowly

lentement, s'il vous plaît.

Numbers

11	12	13	14	15
onze	douze	treize	quatorze	quinze
16	17	18	19	20
seize	dix-sept	dix-huit	dix-neuf	vingt

. . . and to listen out for

Being asked for how many nights/people?

combien de | nuits?
| personnes?

What sort of bed?

un grand lit ou deux lits?

What toilet facilities?

avec bain, douche ou cabinet de toilette?

Your room number

le numéro vingt et un
le numéro soixante et un

Being told on the second, third floor

au deuxième | étage
au troisième |

What the price includes

le prix de la chambre — prix net, taxes et service compris

What name is it?

c'est à quel nom?

Choosing breakfast − to drink?

café	noir?			citron?
	au lait?		thé	au lait?
chocolat?				nature?

. . . and to eat?

avec	pain?
	croissants?

Explanations

Plurals

When there's more than one of anything, there's usually an -s on the end of the word.

Singular	*Plural*
un thé	deux thé*s*
une bière	trois bière*s*

le, la and *l'* become *les* in the plural.

le sandwich	*les* sandwichs
la banque	*les* banques
*l'*orange	*les* oranges

un and *une* become *des* in the plural.

un café	*des* cafés
un hôtel	*des* hôtels
un apéritif	*des* apéritifs
une banque	*des* banques

Some words have a different ending in the plural, e.g. *le journal* becomes *les journaux*.

When there's a vowel or *h* after *les* or *des* pronounce the *s* like *z* to make a smooth link with the next word: *les␣oranges, des␣hôtels*.

Worth knowing

Where to stay

If you can't find a room, the local Tourist Office *(le Syndicat d'Initiative)* will provide a list of accommodation.

Hotel-type accommodation

hôtels	all types from 5-star luxury to modest 1-star
relais de campagne	comfortable, but expensive, country inns
logis de France	moderately priced country hotels, off the beaten track. Lists are available from the appropriate address on page 58.
pensions	simple accommodation, good food, moderately priced
auberges de jeunesse	youth hostels, open to all members of NYHA. Stays are limited to 3-4 nights.

Self-catering holidays

gîtes de France	excellent low-cost accommodation, often in farmhouses and other rural dwellings. Information is available from the appropriate address on page 58.
camping & caravanning	there are many sites, all over France. Useful information can be found in the Michelin Green Guide. It's advisable to get an International Camping Carnet from the AA or RAC.

Out camping

INTERDICTION DE CAMPER ┃
DÉFENSE DE CAMPER ┃ camping prohibited
CAMPING INTERDIT ┃
PROPRIÉTÉ PRIVÉE   private property
PÊCHE INTERDITE   no fishing
COMPLET   no vacancies
un emplacement   a pitch (for tent or caravan)
les douches   showers

Having breakfast

In hotels you may find a little form *(une fiche)*
by the side of your bed to be filled in if you want
breakfast in your room. Tick off the items you want
and hook it over the door handle outside. Breakfast
is usually served from 7-10 am.

Un café complet is a full continental breakfast —
coffee, tea or hot chocolate with *croissants,* soft
rolls *(petits pains)* or French bread with butter and
jam *(confiture)*. If you want marmalade, that's
confiture d'oranges.

Un café au lait is what white coffee is called in the
hotel or in someone's home — otherwise it's
un café crème.

Exercises

1   Read each of the following phrases aloud
several times. Which phrase goes best with which
situation? Write the appropriate number by each one.

a   Lentement, s'il vous plaît . . . . . .
b   Une chambre s'il vous plaît . . . . . .
c   Avec bain . . . . . .
d   Avec pain . . . . . .
e   Avec un grand lit . . . . . .

1   You want a double bed
2   You want a room with a bath
3   The receptionist is speaking too quickly
4   You're looking for a room
5   You'd rather just have bread with your breakfast

2

Imagine you are these people wanting
accommodation at the Hôtel de Bretagne. How do
you answer the receptionist's questions? (see page
57 for 'Days of the week')

Vous	*(First, ask for a room.)* ....
	....
Réceptionniste	Oui, pour combien de personnes?
Vous	....
Réceptionniste	*(a and b only)* Vous désirez un grand lit ou deux lits?
Vous	....
Réceptionniste	Avec bain, avec une douche, ou avec cabinet de toilette?
Vous	....
Réceptionniste	C'est pour combien de nuits? *(Your stay includes the nights of the first and last days.)*
Vous	....

3 You and your family want a room with a bath for four nights. Complete the captions:

a _ _ _ _ _ _ _ _ _ _ _ _

b _ _ _ _ _ _ _ _ _ _ _

c _ _ _ _ _ _ _ _ _ _ _ _

d _ _ _ _ _ _ _ _ _ _

e _ _ _ _ _ _ _ _ _ _ _

f _ _ _ _ _ _ _ _ _ _

4 Practise these numbers:

18	14	11
dix-huit	quatorze	onze

19	16	20
dix-neuf	seize	vingt

5 In the programme you will hear an order for breakfast. Fill in the appropriate numbers and check the answers at the beginning of the next programme.

> La fiche
> Petit déjeuner
> ☐ chocolat(s)
> ☐ café(s) noir
> ☐   au lait
> ☐ thé(s) citron
> ☐   au lait
> ☐   nature
> ☐ avec croissants
> ☐ avec pain

3 Getting your shopping done

Conversations

Buying eggs

Client   Je voudrais <u>six oeufs</u>, s'il vous plaît.
Épicière   Oui . . . voilà monsieur.

. . . a litre of milk

Client   Je voudrais <u>un litre de lait</u>, s'il vous plaît.

. . . wine

Cliente   <u>Un litre de vin blanc.</u>
Épicière   Un litre de vin blanc. Oui, alors, voici madame.

alors, voici   *here you are*

. . . fruit

Cliente   Vous me mettez <u>un kilo de bananes et un kilo de raisins.</u>

vous me mettez   *give me*

. . . butter

Cliente   Je voudrais <u>du beurre.</u>
Épicière   Oui madame, une livre, ou une demi-livre?
Cliente   Eh, oui, <u>une demi-livre.</u>
Épicière   Une demi-livre, oui.

. . . bread

Client   <u>Bonjour madame.</u>
Boulangère   Bonjour monsieur. Vous désirez monsieur?
Client   Je voudrais <u>du pain</u>, s'il vous plaît.

Boulangère	Oui alors, baguette, pain de campagne, ou petite ficelle ?
Client	Eh bien, je peux avoir <u>une demi-baguette</u> ?
Boulangère	Oui, bien sûr, monsieur.
Client	C'est <u>combien</u> ?
Boulangère	Cinquante-cinq centimes.
Client	Voici.
Boulangère	Merci, monsieur.
Client	<u>Merci, au revoir madame.</u>
Boulangère	Au revoir monsieur ; à bientôt monsieur.

baguette *French bread*
pain de campagne *cottage loaf*
petite ficelle *very thin French bread*
je peux avoir *can I have*
voici *here you are*

. . . petrol

Cliente	<u>Bonjour madame.</u>
Pompiste	Bonjour madame.
Cliente	Je voudrais <u>de l'essence</u>, s'il vous plaît.
Pompiste	Ordinaire ou super, madame ?
Cliente	<u>Super.</u>
Pompiste	Pour combien, madame ?
Cliente	Pour <u>quarante francs</u>, s'il vous plaît.
Pompiste	Oui, d'accord, madame.

d'accord *O.K.*

. . . stamps for letters and postcards

Cliente	<u>Bonjour madame.</u>
Employée	Bonjour madame.
Cliente	Je voudrais <u>des timbres</u>, s'il vous plaît.
Employée	Oui, c'est pour quelle destination ?
Cliente	Pour <u>l'Angleterre</u>.
Employée	Pour la Grande Bretagne. Vous avez lettres et cartes postales ?

Cliente	<u>Deux lettres.</u>
Employée	Deux lettres. Et les cartes postales?
Cliente	<u>Cinq cartes postales.</u>
Employée	Alors un franc par carte postale et un franc quarante par lettre.

par carte postale *for each postcard*

. . . and an English newspaper

Une femme	<u>Bonjour madame.</u>
Vendeuse	Bonjour madame.
Une femme	Je voudrais <u>un journal anglais,</u> <u>s'il vous plaît.</u>
Vendeuse	Je n'ai pas de journaux anglais. Vous allez trouver ça Place de la Mairie.
Une femme	Bien, <u>merci.</u>

vous allez trouver ça *you'll find some*

What you'll need to say during the programme . . .

Saying how many you want

six oeufs	
un journal anglais	s'il vous plaît
une (demi-) baguette	

Saying how much you want

un litre	de	lait
deux litres		vin blanc/rouge/rosé
un kilo	de	bananes
deux kilos		raisins
une demi-livre de beurre		

How to say 'some . . .'

du beurre   de l'essence
    des timbres

Saying where your postcards are for

Grande Bretagne

. . . and to listen out for

What weight?
une livre ou une demi-livre?

What sort of bread?
baguette, pain de campagne, ou petite ficelle?

Are they letters or postcards?
vous avez lettres et cartes postales?

For which country?
pour quelle destination?

What grade of petrol?
ordinaire ou super?

They haven't got what you want
je *n'*ai *pas* (de journaux anglais)

Numbers: 21-60

	21	30
	vingt et un	trente
40	50	60
quarante	cinquante	soixante

You can find more details on pages 56/57.

Explanations

How to say 'some' or 'any' . . .

When 'some' or 'any' means more than one, use
    des — *des* sandwichs, *des* timbres.

When it means a quantity of, use
    du in front of masculine words — *du* beurre
    de la in front of feminine words — *de la* soupe
    de l' in front of words beginning with a vowel
       or *h* — (changer) *de l'* argent

Worth knowing

Shopping for food

Most towns in France have at least one supermarket *(un supermarché)* where you can buy most things and outside large towns you'll often find a hypermarket *(un hypermarché)* where you can buy almost anything. But for fresh vegetables, meat and fish try the local market *(le marché)* where things tend to be fresher. Most food shops close on Mondays but some, notably bakeries and cake shops, are open on Sunday mornings.

Bread is best bought fresh every day from the baker's *(la boulangerie)*. A stick of French bread is called *une baguette*. You can buy just half *(une demi-baguette)* and there are also soft rolls *(des petits pains)* or, most like English white bread, *pain de mie*. The nearest to brown bread is *pain complet*.

When you're out shopping for food other shop signs you could come across are:

ALIMENTATION ÉPICERIE	food and groceries
BOUCHERIE	meat
FROMAGERIE	cheese
LAITERIE	dairy produce
LIBRE SERVICE	small supermarket
PÂTISSERIE	cakes and pastries

Weights and quantities

un kilogramme (1000 grammes)=2.2 lbs.
un demi-kilo (also called *une livre*)=just over 1 lb.
250 (deux cent cinquante) grammes=about ½ lb.
100 (cent) grammes=about 4 ozs.
un litre=just under two pints
cinq litres=just over a gallon
un demi-litre=about one pint

a little of	*un peu de . . .*
a slice of	*une tranche de . . .*
a tin of	*une boîte de . . .*

a bottle of   *une bouteille de* . . .
a packet of   *un paquet de* . . .
a tube of   *un tube de* . . .

> . . . with the name of whatever you want, e.g.
> *quatre tranches de jambon*
> *deux bouteilles d'orangeade*

Buying newspapers, stamps and cigarettes

Newspapers   can be bought from newspaper kiosks and you should be able to buy English ones, at a price, in large towns.

Stamps   can be bought at the Post Office *(PTT, P et T, la poste)* and also at *bureaux de tabac* and bars displaying the traditional red sign outside. You may be able to get them at your hotel or where you buy your postcards.

red

Cigarettes and tobacco   are also available where you see the red sign. English brands, if they have them, will be expensive. For mild cigarettes, ask for *des blondes*. French cigarettes are *des brunes,* and are fairly strong.

Postal services

Post Office   *(la poste* – recognised by the sign *PTT* or *P et T).* The usual services are open from 8 am-7 pm, Monday-Friday, and from 8 am-12 noon on Saturdays.

Letterboxes   are yellow in France and Switzerland, red in Belgium. When there's more than one slot post your letters or postcards in the right one:
LETTRES   Inland letters and postcards

| ÉTRANGER | Letters and postcards for abroad |
| IMPRIMÉS | Printed matter |

Telephones You can make calls from the Post Office, from a café or from a public booth (though there are fewer in France than in the U.S.). Public telephones take 20 centime coins: put them in before you dial. They drop through automatically when your call is connected, and any unused ones are returned when you hang up. The code for international calls from France is 19; wait for a second dial tone, then dial 11 for the U.S. So, to call a number, dial 19, wait for signal, 11, area code, phone number.

Banks

In large towns banks are generally open from
Monday-Friday: 9 am-12 noon and 2 pm-4 pm.
Saturday: 9.30 am-12 noon (during the tourist season).
In small towns banks are closed on Mondays instead of Saturday afternoons.
All banks are closed on Sundays and Public Holidays.
The *franc* is the unit of currency in France. There are 100 *centimes* to the *franc*.

Chemists

A green neon cross is displayed outside the shop. Chemists are usually qualified to treat minor ailments and injuries.

Public conveniences

Few and far between — especially for ladies!

Les toilettes:
DAMES   Ladies   LIBRE   Vacant
HOMMES   Gentlemen OCCUPÉ   Engaged
The sign 'WC' indicates that the facilities are shared.

Motoring

The car won't go! — *La voiture ne marche pas!*
You'll need *un garage*. If you know which bit isn't working and the name of it, just say: . . . . . . *ne marche pas!* You don't know the name? Point to it and say: *ça ne marche pas!*

For oil *(de l'huile),* water *(de l'eau)* and petrol *(de l'essence)* you can go to *une station service.* Petrol grades are *ordinaire/normale*=2 star, *super*=4 star.

You can buy petrol
— by the litre: *(vingt) litres, s'il vous plaît*
— by francs' worth: *(quarante) francs, s'il vous plaît*
— by asking 'fill her up': *le plein, s'il vous plaît*

At a self-service station, the instructions will be similar to these.
1 *Décrochez le pistolet et engagez-le dans votre réservoir.*
   (Remove nozzle from holster and place in petrol tank.)
2 *Vérifiez que les compteurs sont à zéro.*
   (Make sure all meters are at zero.)
3 *Servez-vous.*
   (Fill as required.)
4 *Raccrochez le pistolet.*
   (Replace nozzle in holster.)
5 *Présentez-vous à la caisse.*
   (Pay the cashier.)

Exercises

1 You're shopping for food on your self-catering holiday. Here is your shopping list. How would you ask for each item? Say it out loud, then write it down in French.

Price

6 eggs	....	....
1 litre of milk	....	....
½ pound of butter	....	....
1 kilo of bananas	....	....
1 kilo of oranges	....	....
4 slices of ham	....	....
1 packet of biscuits	....	....
1 baguette	....	....
12 soft rolls	....	....

TOTAL

Then work out what your shopping will cost, using the prices below as a guide:

lait	*un franc quatre-vingt-cinq le litre*
oeufs	*six francs quarante la douzaine* (dozen)
oranges	*trois francs cinquante le kilo*
bananes	*trois francs le kilo*
baguette	*un franc dix*
beurre	*cinq francs la demi-livre*
biscuits	*trois francs cinquante le paquet*
petits pains	*un franc vingt la pièce* (each)
jambon	*six francs les 4 tranches* (slices)

2 Work out the rest of this conversation at the baker's shop.

La boulangère	Bonjour monsieur/madame/ mademoiselle.
Vous	*(She's an elderly lady.)* ....
La boulangère	Vous désirez?
Vous	*(Tell her you'd like a baguette, five croissants and five rolls.)* ....
La boulangère	Alors ça fait un franc dix la baguette et cinq francs les croissants, plus six

francs les petits pains. Ce qui vous
fait douze francs dix en tout.

Vous   *(That was all a bit fast. Ask her to
speak slowly.)* ....

La boulangère   Ça fait douze francs dix centimes en
tout, s'il vous plaît.
(Write the price here.) ....

Vous   *(Thank her, and when you have paid,
say goodbye.)* ....
....

ça fait   *that's*   ce qui vous fait   *which makes*

3   Where are you likely to be if the following
things are said to you? Choose from this list:
    la poste / une station service
    une banque / une boulangerie
a   Ordinaire ou super? ....
b   C'est pour quelle destination? ....
c   Alors une baguette, pain de campagne ou petite
    ficelle? ....
d   En quelle monnaie? ....

4   Complete this conversation:
Vous   *(Ask for some stamps)* ....
....

Employée   C'est pour quelle destination?
Vous   *(Great Britain)* ....
Employée   Vous avez lettres et cartes postales?
Vous   *(1 letter and 4 postcards)* ....
....

Employée   Alors ça fait cinq francs quarante.
(Write down how much.) ....

5   Read these prices aloud, and write down in
figures what they are:
a   quatorze francs vingt   ....
b   quarante francs cinquante   ....
c   quatre francs soixante   ....
d   vingt-quatre francs quarante   ....
e   seize francs cinquante-cinq   ....

4 Getting around

Conversations

Looking for a car park

Un touriste	<u>S'il vous plaît,</u> où y a-t-il <u>un parking?</u>
Un homme	Un parking, bien, il y en a un qui est assez important. C'est sur votre gauche à cinquante mètres environ. Vous allez le voir, hein, de toute manière.
Un touriste	Très bien, <u>merci monsieur.</u>

il y en a un qui est assez important   *there's quite a large one*
vous allez le voir de toute manière   *you'll see it anyway*

. . . the post office

Un touriste	<u>S'il vous plaît monsieur,</u> où est <u>la poste?</u>
Un homme	La poste, alors, vous allez tout droit, vous tournez à gauche, vous descendez, et vous prendrez la première à droite.

vous allez *go*   vous descendez *go down*
vous tournez *turn*   vous prendrez *take*

. . . the town centre

Un touriste	Pardon madame, <u>le centre de la ville,</u> <u>s'il vous plaît?</u>
Une femme	Ah, c'est compliqué. Pour cela il vaut mieux que vous preniez le bus. Vous prenez la première rue à droite, et là tout de suite vous avez un bus.

il vaut mieux que vous preniez le bus   *you'd be better taking the bus*
là tout de suite   *just there*

Looking for the Place de la Mairie

Un touriste	<u>S'il vous plait monsieur, la Place de la Mairie?</u>
Un homme	Alors, la Place de la Mairie, c'est simple, hein! Vous allez tout droit, aux deuxième feux vous tournez à droite et vous allez voir une grande place.

aux deuxième feux   *at the second set of traffic lights*
vous allez voir une grande place   *you'll see a large square*

. . . a restaurant

Un touriste	<u>S'il vous plaît mademoiselle,</u> est-ce qu'il y a <u>un restaurant</u> près d'ici?
Une femme	Je ne sais pas, je ne suis pas d'ici.

près d'ici   *near here*
je ne sais pas, je ne suis pas d'ici   *I don't know, I'm not from around here.*

. . . the Syndicat d'Initiative

Un touriste	<u>S'il vous plaît monsieur, le Syndicat d'Initiative?</u>
Un homme	Le Syndicat d'Initiative, c'est très facile à trouver. Vous allez tourner à gauche au bout de cette rue, et descendre en passant deux feux.

c'est très facile à trouver   *it's very easy to find*
au bout de cette rue   *at the end of this street*
descendre en passant deux feux   *go down past two sets of traffic lights*

. . . the Palais de Justice?

Un touriste	<u>S'il vous plaît madame, le Palais de Justice?</u>
L'hôtesse	*(showing the way on a map)* Vous allez continuer tout droit, et prendre la deuxième rue sur votre gauche.

Un touriste	Oui.
L'hôtesse	Vous allez remonter tout droit jusqu'à la Place du Palais, et c'est sur cette place qu'est le Palais de Justice.

c'est sur cette place qu'est le Palais de Justice
the Palais de Justice is in this square.

. . . and the station
Un homme	La gare, non, non, non, vous êtes dans la direction opposée. Vous allez retourner, d'où vous venez, et retourner à gauche au bout de la rue, et après descendre tout droit et vous allez trouver la gare.

d'où vous venez   *where you've come from*

Buying a train ticket to Paris
Voyageur	Bonjour monsieur, je voudrais un billet pour Paris, s'il vous plaît.
Employé	Oui, en seconde classe?
Voyageur	En seconde classe, oui.
Employé	Alors, ça sera soixante-dix francs, monsieur.
Voyageur	Très bien, voici. *(gives him the money)*
Employé	Merci monsieur.

je voudrais un billet pour Paris   *I'd like a ticket for Paris*
alors, ça sera . . .   *let's see, that'll be . . .*
très bien, voici   *right, here you are*

. . . and to Bordeaux
Voyageur	Pour aller à Bordeaux, s'il vous plaît?
Employé	Oui alors, c'est quatre-vingt-dix-sept francs, monsieur. Aller simple, ou aller-retour?
Voyageur	Aller-retour.

| *Employé* | Aller-retour. Alors le prochain train est à seize heures dix-neuf. |

le prochain train   *the next train*

What you'll need to say during the programme . . .

Asking the way

| s'il vous plaît | monsieur madame mademoiselle | un supermarché? un parking? le Syndicat d'Initiative? la gare? |

Getting a map
un plan de la ville, s'il vous plaît.

Getting the right train ticket

Paris, please	Paris s'il vous plaît
second class	en seconde classe
single — return	aller simple — aller-retour
for one	une personne

. . . and to listen out for

Directions   tout droit
                     straight on

à gauche   à droite
to the left   *to the right*

on the/your left   *on the/your right*
sur la/votre gauche   ←——→   sur la/votre droite
la première à gauche   la deuxième à droite
first left   *second right*

Numbers: 60-100
For example:

60	70
soixante	soixante-dix
80	90	100
quatre-vingts	quatre-vingt-dix	cent

Explanations

Understanding the time

It's not necessary to be able to *tell* anyone the time, but you'll need to *understand* what other people are saying when they tell you the time!

1 o'clock – une heure
2 o'clock – deux heures
3 o'clock – trois heures
4 o'clock – quatre heures
12 o'clock – douze heures
or *midday* – midi
   midnight – minuit
1.05 – une heure cinq
2.10 – deux heures dix
3.15 – trois heures │ quinze
                │ et quart
4.30 – quatre heures │ trente
                │ et demie
5.40 – │ cinq heures quarante
      │ six heures moins vingt
6.45 – │ six heures quarante-cinq
      │ sept heures moins le quart

The twenty four hour clock system is used for giving times of public transport, public performances, etc., so you will hear *treize heures* for 1 pm, *quatorze heures* for 2 pm etc.

in the morning – le matin   *today* – aujourd'hui
in the afternoon – l'après midi   *tomorrow* – demain
in the evening – le soir

For names of months and days of weeks, see page 57.

Finding the way

Listen out for these words when you ask the way . . .
Landmarks

le carrefour *crossroads*   le pont *bridge*
le rond-point *roundabout*   le coin *corner*
les feux *traffic lights*   le panneau *signpost*
l'église *church*

Directions

tournez *turn*	montez *go up*
prenez *take*	descendez *go down*
continuez *carry on*	passez devant *go past*
traversez *cross*	au bout *to the end*

Worth knowing

Getting around by car

Roads are classified on maps as:

A   *autoroute* – motorway – on which you normally have to pay a toll *(un péage)*

N   *route nationale* – main road

D   *route départementale* – pleasanter and less crowded road

Quieter routes are indicated by green arrows on a white background and called *Itinéraires Bis*. Unless otherwise indicated vehicles coming from the right have right of way.

Priority to traffic from the right

You have priority

Parking   Most towns have *zones bleues* – parking in specified places for a certain length of time. You can get a parking disc *(disque bleu* or *disque de stationnement)* from the police station, *bureaux de tabac* or *stations service*. There are also parking meters *(parc-mètres)* similar to ours.

Seat belts	If your car is fitted with them they must be worn all the time, except in town during the daytime and early evening.
Street signs	Some of the most common are:

STATIONNEMENT INTERDIT
no parking
ACCÈS INTERDIT ⎫
ENTRÉE INTERDITE ⎬ no entry
SENS UNIQUE   one way
DÉVIATION   diversion
CÔTÉ DE STATIONNEMENT
parking on this side
PRIORITÉ À DROITE   priority to
traffic from the right
TRAVAUX   roadworks

Public transport

Train French Rail (SNCF) has special concessions for parties, students, and pensioners. Children up to 4 travel free; those between 4-10 pay half fare.

Types of train
TEE   – *Trans-Europ Express, with supplementary fare.*
rapide   – *express train, with supplementary fare.*
express   – *fast train, stops only at main stations.*
omnibus – *local train, stops at all stations.*
autorail – *small diesel for short runs.*

Station notices
ACCÈS AUX QUAIS   to the platforms
ARRIVÉES   arrivals
BILLETS   tickets
CONSIGNE   left luggage
DÉFENSE DE CRACHER   no spitting
DÉFENSE DE FUMER   no smoking
DÉPARTS   departures

EAU POTABLE drinking water
ENTRÉE way in
FERMÉ closed
OBJETS TROUVÉS lost property
OUVERT open
PASSAGE SOUTERRAIN subway
POUSSEZ push
RENSEIGNEMENTS enquiries
SALLE D'ATTENTE waiting room
SORTIE way out
TIREZ pull

Underground *Le Métro* – is only found in Paris and Lyons. It's the cheapest way to get around – buy a book of tickets *(un carnet)* if you intend to use it frequently.

Bus and coach timetables and details can be obtained from *le Syndicat d'Initiative* or the bus station *(la gare routière)*.

Taxi you'll need to go to a taxi rank *(une tête de station)* or telephone for one. They normally arrive within a few minutes.

On foot

In town Use pedestrian crossings when possible. Watch the illuminated signs:
ATTENDEZ PIÉTONS wait
PASSEZ PIÉTONS cross now

Hitch hiking Not illegal, but not encouraged.

Rambling There are many signposted tracks for ramblers. Routes are also marked on maps. More details are available from *Le Comité National des sentiers de grande randonnée,* 92 rue de Clignancourt, 75883, Paris.

Exercises

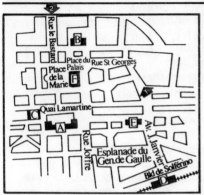

Key to map
A la poste (PTT)
B le Palais de Justice
C le Syndicat d'Initiative
D la gare (SNCF)
E le musée *(museum)*
F le théâtre

(You will also need to refer to the map when you listen to this programme.)

1 Starting from the points indicated, follow the directions and say where you get to.

a *Starting from point 1.* Vous tournez à gauche, vous continuez tout droit jusqu'à la Place de la Mairie. Vous tournez à gauche, et aprés à droite et .... est sur votre gauche.

b *Starting from point 2.* Vous descendez la rue le Bastard. Vous traversez la Place de la Mairie; vous continuez tout droit et vous arrivez Quai Lamartine. Prenez à gauche. Continuez tout droit, jusqu'à l'Avenue J. Janvier. Prenez à droite et .... est sur votre droite.

c *Starting from the railway station.* Montez l'Avenue J. Janvier. Prenez la quatrième à gauche. Continuez tout droit jusqu'à la Rue Joffre. Tournez à gauche, puis prenez à droite, et .... est sur votre droite.

d *Starting from le Palais de Justice.* Traversez la Place du Palais. Tournez à gauche et prenez la rue St Georges. Prenez la deuxième à droite, et vous descendez l'Avenue J. Janvier jusqu'à ....

2 CONSIGNE
   BUREAU DE CHANGE *(see Word list)*
   RENSEIGNEMENTS
   TABAC *(see page 29)*
   ATTENDEZ PIÉTONS
   ACCÈS AUX QUAIS
   PASSAGE SOUTERRAIN
   ÉTRANGER *(see page 30)*
   EAU POTABLE

Which of the above notices might you see when doing the following things?

a   crossing the station via the subway ....
b   buying stamps and postcards ....
c   posting your cards to England ....
d   making your way to your train ....
e   leaving your luggage in a locker ....
f   changing money ....
g   getting information about train times ....
h   having a drink of water from a drinking fountain
    ....
i   waiting to cross the road ....

3 To practise recognising departure times when they are given to you, write down these times, stating whether a.m. or p.m.

a   quinze heures dix ....
b   dix-huit heures quinze ....
c   huit heures cinq ....
d   dix-neuf heures cinquante-neuf ....
e   vingt-trois heures douze ....
f   six heures quarante-cinq ....
g   seize heures trente-deux ....
h   dix heures vingt-cinq ....
i   onze heures treize ....
j   treize heures onze ....

Test your skill

Prepare these exercises before listening to
programme five and check the answers with
Bénédicte and Daniel during the programme.

1 Getting to know people
What do you say when you're asked:
a Comment allez-vous? ....
b Ça va? ....
c *How do you say hello when it's evening?*
....

2 Finding somewhere to stay

Vous	*(Tell the receptionist you've booked a room.)* ....
Réceptionniste	Pour combien de personnes?
Vous	*(Say it's for two people.)* ....
Réceptionniste	Oui, quel nom.
Vous	*(Give your name.)* .... *(Ask how much it is.)* ....
Réceptionniste	Soixante-dix francs.
Vous	*(Ask her to repeat it.)* ....
Réceptionniste	Soixante-dix francs.

3 Going shopping
Complete this conversation:

Vous	*(Ask for five stamps.)* ....
Employée	Pour quelle destination?
Vous	*(Tell her they're going to Great Britain.)* ....
Employée	Lettres ou cartes postales?
Vous	*(Tell her: postcards.)* ....

| *Employée* | Alors, cinq francs, s'il vous plaît. |
| *Vous* | *(Say thank you.)* .... |

4 Getting around

a *How do you ask this lady the way to the toilets (les toilettes)?* ....

b *What are these directions you're given?*
'A droite et à gauche'.................................

c | *Vous* | *(Tell the ticket clerk you want to go to Paris.)* .... |
Employé	En seconde classe?
Vous	*(Say yes.)* ....
Employé	Aller simple ou aller-retour?
Vous	*(Ask for a return, please.)* ....
	....

5 Getting by with numbers

Room numbers

soixante et un ....
quatre-vingt-douze ....
quarante-cinq ....
trente-huit ....

Prices

cinquante-cinq centimes ....
vingt-cinq francs ....
trente-neuf francs ....
quatre-vingts centimes ....

5 Getting a meal out

Conversations

Asking for the menu

Cliente Vous avez la carte, s'il vous plaît?
Serveuse Non madame, nous ne faisons qu'un menu.

nous ne faisons qu'un menu *we only serve a set meal*

Choosing an apéritif

Serveuse Ricard, Pernod, Raphaël, Martini, Cinzano, Cinquante et un?

Saying how you like your meat

Serveuse Comment aimez-vous vos viandes, à point, saignantes, bleues?

comment aimez-vous vos viandes? *how do you like your meat?*

Serveuse Comment les voulez-vous? À point, bien cuits, saignants?
Cliente Un saignant et un à point.
Serveuse Un à point, d'accord, entendu, madame.

comment les voulez-vous? *how do you like them (your steaks)?*

Ordering a set meal

Serveuse Et c'est quinze francs le menu plus la boisson.
Cliente Alors deux menus.
Serveuse Deux menus.

plus la boisson *drinks extra*

Choosing vegetables

Serveuse	Et en légumes que prendrez-vous? Vous avez frites, salade, flageolets.
Cliente	<u>Salade.</u>
Serveuse	Une salade, et madame?
Cliente	<u>Des flageolets.</u>
Serveuse	Des flageolets: des flageolets et une salade.

que prendrez-vous? *what will you have?*

Being offered a choice of dessert

Serveuse	Vous avez différents desserts; vous avez des glaces, des fruits, pâtisseries maison, pêche melba.

Finding the toilets!

Serveuse	C'est dans le fond de la cour. Vous prenez à droite et à gauche.

c'est dans le fond de la cour *they're on the far side of the courtyard*

What you'll need to say during the programme . . .

Asking for the menu
la carte, s'il vous plaît

. . . or a set meal

un			
deux	menu(s)	à quinze francs	s'il vous plaît
trois		à vingt francs	

. . . and the bill
l'addition, s'il vous plaît

Ordering something to eat

un steak	des flageolets
une salade	une pêche melba
des frites	une pâtisserie maison

How you'd like your meat

bien cuit   saignant
à point   bleu

. . . and to listen out for

We only serve set meals
nous ne faisons qu'un menu
Drinks extra
plus la boisson
A choice of dessert
des glaces, des fruits, pâtisseries maison, pêche melba

Explanations

Adjectives

Most adjectives come after the nouns they describe, but there are some frequently used ones which come before: e.g.
un journal *anglais*
un disque *bleu*   but   une *grande* place

Adjectives which describe a feminine word usually take an *e* on the end to 'agree' with the noun: e.g.
une femme fatal*e*   une petite ficel*e*

If more than one feminine thing is being described you usually add *es* to the adjective: e.g.
des cigarettes anglais*es*

If more than one masculine thing is being described, you usually just add *s* to the adjective: e.g.
deux steaks saignant*s*

Worth knowing

Eating out

For good value try *le menu touristique,* a set meal with a choice of main dishes. There's also the expensive *menu gastronomique* for gourmets. Otherwise the set meal is just called *le menu.*
It often works out more expensive to eat *à la carte.*

What's on the menu?

Potage/soupe Soup	*consommé* clear, often chilled *bouillon* broth: *velouté* cream:
Hors d'oeuvres Starters	*crudités* grated raw vegetables with French dressing *charcuterie* cold cooked meats *terrine* potted meat
Entrées	*cuisses de grenouille* frog's legs *escargots* snails: *raviolis* ravioli
Viande Meat	*bifteck/steak* steak: *boeuf* beef *gibier* game: *entrecôte* rib of beef *mouton/gigot/agneau* lamb *porc* pork: *poulet* chicken *veau* veal: *volaille* poultry
Légumes Vegetables	*choux* cabbage: *épinards* spinach *flageolets* kidney beans: *frites* chips *haricots* beans: *petits pois* peas *pommes de terre* potatoes *salade* lettuce with vinaigrette dressing
Fromage Cheese	A wide range, and served before dessert. The most common are Roquefort, Camembert, Gruyère and Brie, but try one you don't know!
Dessert	No heavy puddings or pies! It could be a selection of: *glaces* ice cream *pêche melba* peach melba *pâtisseries* cakes and pastries *crème caramel* cream caramel

Some menu terms

which describe how something is prepared

lyonnais	with onions
à l'anglaise	boiled
provençal	with tomatoes, garlic, anchovies, herbs
florentine	with spinach

mornay   with cheese sauce
au gratin   with cheese sauce and baked in the oven.

Wines

A vast selection! *Un vin blanc/rouge/rosé* will get
you the local wine and *vin ordinaire* is everyday,
or local, wine. If you want a better one, look for
the words *appellation contrôlée* or the letters
VDQS *(vin délimité de qualité supérieure)*.

Hidden extras

Pain et couvert   the 'cover charge' which is
often added to the bill.
TVA = VAT
TTC (toutes taxes comprises) = all taxes included.
Service compris   means there's no more to pay. But
although 15%-20% service is included it's usual to
round up your bill to the nearest franc.

Tips on tipping

Hotels   even if the bill says *service compris,* the
porter and chambermaid generally expect a tip.
About 5F *(francs)* for the chambermaid (10-20F
in a big hotel) and 1-2F for the porter (5-10F
in a big hotel).
Taxi drivers   2-3F.
Cinema/theatre usherettes   about 2F.
Lavatory attendant   a few centimes if you're a man.
A few more if you're a lady.
Guides   about 1F per person when you're in a party.
Hairdressers   at your own discretion.
Petrol station   if your windows are cleaned or
tyre pressures checked then give up to 5F.

Exercises

A chance to practise what you've learned in all the
five programmes!
1   You and your wife/husband are on your way
to a camp-site when your car breaks down, so you
have to find a hotel just for the night. You've
been directed to the Hôtel de Bretagne.

Vous	*(Say good evening to the young lady receptionist. Ask for a room.)*
	....
	....
Réceptionniste	Pour combien de personnes?
Vous	....
Réceptionniste	Avec un grand lit ou deux lits?
Vous	*(Say you want a double bed.)* ......
	....
Réceptionniste	Pour combien de nuits?
Vous	....

2 That evening you have a meal in a nearby restaurant:

a Ask for two set meals at 15 francs. ....
....

b You both choose steak: you like yours well done, and with chips and salad, but your husband/wife likes it rare, with just salad. ....
....

c After your meal, order one black coffee and one white coffee. ....

3 Next morning after breakfast, you decide to go and spend the day exploring Rouen until the car's ready. You're going by train, and you want two returns.

Vous	*(First state your destination.)* ....
....
Employé	Aller simple ou aller-retour?
Vous	....
Employé	Pour combien de personnes?
Vous	....
Employé	En seconde classe?
Vous	*(Say yes.)* ....
Employé	Cinquante-quatre francs soixante.
Vous	*(You didn't quite catch the price. Ask him to speak slowly, please)* ....
....

4 When the time comes to get your train back, you're not sure of the way back to the station.
Vous (Ask this man.) ....
Now follow the directions given you, starting at the arrow.

Monsieur Tournez à gauche, et continuez jusqu'à la rue Jeanne d'Arc. Tournez à droite et continuez tout droit, et vous arrivez à la gare!

Where is the station, A B or C?

5 a Your car is ready when you get back. You pay the bill then realise you need petrol.
Vous (Tell the attendant you want to fill up)
....
Pompiste Ordinaire ou super?
Vous (Tell her you want four star.) ....
b You finally get to the camp-site. You haven't booked. How do you ask if there's a site available?.....................................
c Next day you need to go shopping for food. There's a shop on the site which sells most things. Here's your list. Ask for these items?

12 bread rolls	....
½ lb butter	....
½ litre of milk	....
1 kilo of grapes	....
6 eggs	....

6 a Holiday's over! You're heading for the coast. There's no hurry, and you prefer a scenic route. Which type of road will you choose?
A.............. N.............. D..............
b Every so often, you come across a triangular road-sign saying PASSAGE PROTÉGÉ.
What does it mean?.....................................

Reference section

Extra language notes

Verbs   Depending on who is doing the action, and when it takes place, the ending of the verb changes. You may have noticed already that the ending -*ez* usually goes with *vous,* but *je* and *nous* take different endings. Some parts of some verbs are not used very often, so just learn to say and recognise the parts which are immediately useful to you. The word list at the back of the book gives parts of verbs as they appear in the programmes but in dictionaries, you usually find just the infinitive of the verb, e.g. *continuer* = to continue.

Negatives   You may not always be able to get what you want. You can usually tell this from the look on the assistant's face, but listen out for *non* and *ne(n')* . . . *pas*. e.g.
Non, je *n'*ai *pas* de journaux anglais.
Je *ne* suis *pas* d'ici.

Pronunciation guide

First of all try to impersonate a French person speaking English with a very heavy French accent. This will help you get used to hearing yourself make some of the different sounds you'll use when speaking French. The best way to acquire a good French accent is to listen to and imitate the real-life French you hear in the programmes. Imitate the rhythm and intonation of words and phrases as closely as possible when you are invited to 'have a go' in the pauses.

The following brief guide to French pronunciation will be useful when you are reading through the conversations and when you come across unfamiliar words for the first time. Only sounds which are very different from English are given below. The English equivalents are approximate.

Vowels

a/â	similar to 'a' in 'what'	madame, banane pâté
au / eau	similar to 'o' in 'mole'	restaurant
e	is variable, depending on its position, and what letters follow:	
	— on its own, it is like 'a' in 'about'	le, se, ne
	— when followed by two consonants not including 'm' or 'n' it is like 'e' in 'get'	destination
	— when found between two consonants it is sometimes swallowed or elided	mad(e)moiselle
	— at the end of a word it is often not pronounced	douch(e) orang(e)
	— er, ez, et, are similar to 'ay' in 'payment'	aller voulez, billet
è	similar to 'e' in 'them'	crème vous êtes
ê		apéritif désirez
é	similar to 'ay' in 'payment'. Corners of mouth should be pulled well back into a smile for this sound!	
eu	similar to 'u' in 'fur'. Push your lips forward for this sound.	monsieur, deux
i	similar to 'i' in 'police' — lips pulled back tightly!	frites, livre, kilo
o	similar to 'aw' in 'saw'. At the end of a word, similar to 'o' in 'most'.	chocolat kilo
ô	similar to 'o' in 'most'	allô, hôtel

ou	similar to 'oo' in 'food' but the tongue is further back in the mouth and the lips are well rounded	bonjour, bouteille
oi	similar to the first sound in Standard English 'wonder'	au revoir, noir
u	similar to 'oo' in 'food' but pronounced by rounding the lips as in whistling with a high note. With the lips still in that position, try to say *ee* as in 'feet'.	une, brune
ui	similar to English 'wee' in 'week', but shorter	nuit, fruit

Nasal vowels are vowels followed by *m* or *n*. Talk through your nose for these sounds!

-am -an *-em -en*	try saying 'darn' through your nose, lips relaxed and slightly apart, but don't let the tip of your tongue come up to the roof of your mouth for the 'n'.	camping, franc, employé, cent
-on -om	try making the sound above, but with lips pushed right forward, and tongue right back in your mouth.	combien, bonjour
-in -im	lips pulled tightly back as when smiling. Say the name 'Anne' without letting the tip of your tongue touch the roof of your mouth.	impossible, timbre, vin
-un	similar to the previous sound, but with less of a smile! Many French speakers nowadays pronounce this the same as the French *'in'*.	un

Consonants

A consonant in a final position is often not pronounced at all: e.g.
fran(c), anglai(s), Pari(s)

ç	always as 's' in 'soap'	français, ça
ch	like 'sh' in 'shock'	chocolat, changer, douche
g	– in front of 'e' and 'i' it is soft like the 's' in 'treasure'	gite, garage
	– in front of other letters it is hard like the 'g' in 'get'	cigarette, gauche, grand
	– 'gn' sounds like the 'n' in 'newt' or 'union'	champignon, Bretagne
h	is not pronounced	(h)uit, (h)ôtel
j	is pronounced as the soft 'g' above	je, bonjour
ll	– when preceded by an 'i' it is usually pronounced like 'y' in 'yacht'	billet
	– in some words it is pronounced as 'l' in 'feel'	ville, mille
qu	is always like 'k' in 'kick'	que, quatre,
th	is like 't' in 'tell'	thé, théâtre
w	is pronounced like 'v'	

Numbers

0	zéro	10	dix	20	vingt
1	un	11	onze	21	vingt et un
2	deux	12	douze	22	vingt-deux
3	trois	13	treize	23	vingt-trois
4	quatre	14	quatorze	24	vingt-quatre
5	cinq	15	quinze	30	trente
6	six	16	seize	40	quarante
7	sept	17	dix-sept	50	cinquante
8	huit	18	dix-huit	60	soixante
9	neuf	19	dix-neuf	70	soixante-dix

71	soixante et onze	81	quatre-vingt-un
72	soixante-douze	82	quatre-vingt-deux
73	soixante-treize	83	quatre-vingt-trois
74	soixante-quatorze	84	quatre-vingt-quatre
75	soixante-quinze	90	quatre-vingt-dix
76	soixante-seize	91	quatre-vingt-onze
77	soixante-dix-sept	92	quatre-vingt-douze
78	soixante-dix-huit	93	quatre-vingt-treize
79	soixante-dix-neuf	94	quatre-vingt-quatorze
80	quatre-vingts		
100	cent	200	deux cents
101	cent un	500	cinq cents
102	cent deux	1,000	mille
	etc.		

| 1st | premier, première | 3rd | troisième |
| 2nd | deuxième | 4th | quatrième |

In Belgium *septante, octante* and *nonante* replace *soixante-dix, quatre-vingts* and *quatre-vingt-dix*. In Switzerland it is *septante, huitante* and *nonante*. To give yourself extra practice in recognising numbers when they are said, cover up the figures in any one column, read off any number and work out what it is before checking your answer. Better still, work with someone else and test each other.

Days of the week

lundi	Monday	vendredi	Friday
mardi	Tuesday	samedi	Saturday
mercredi	Wednesday	dimanche	Sunday
jeudi	Thursday		

Months of the year

janvier	January	juillet	July
février	February	août	August
mars	March	septembre	September
avril	April	octobre	October
mai	May	novembre	November
juin	June	décembre	December

Useful addresses

French Embassy (cultural services)
972 Fifth Avenue
New York, NY 10021
Tel: (212) 570-4400

French Government Tourist Office
610 Fifth Avenue
New York, NY 10020
Tel: (212) 757-1125

U.S. Student Travel Service, Inc.
801 Second Avenue
New York, NY 10017
Tel: (212) 867-8770

Tours Specialists Inc.
1440 Broadway
New York, NY 10018
Tel: (212) 840-4356

Key to exercises

Programme numéro un

1 (a) S'il vous plaît!

(c) Merci madame

(b) Une bière et un sandwich
au jambon

(d) Au revoir madame

2 (a) Bonjour monsieur
Au revoir monsieur
Merci monsieur

(c) Bonjour Monsieur Giraud
Au revoir Monsieur Giraud
Merci Monsieur Giraud

(b) Bonjour mademoiselle
Au revoir mademoiselle
Merci mademoiselle

(d) Bonjour madame
Au revoir madame
Merci madame

3 un croque-monsieur
un hot dog
un sandwich au fromage
un sandwich au jambon
deux sandwichs au pâté

deux bières
un café noir
deux limonades
un thé nature
un thé au lait
un thé citron

4 (a) Bonjour Monsieur
Leblanc
(c) S'il vous plaît
(e) Ça va merci

(b) Trés bien merci

(d) Merci!
(f) Au revoir Monsieur Leblanc

Programme numéro deux

1 a(3) b(4) c(2) d(5) e(1)

2 Une chambre s'il vous plaît
- (a) deux personnes / deux lits / avec bain / trois nuits
- (b) deux personnes / un grand lit / avec une douche / quatre nuits
- (c) une personne / avec cabinet de toilette / une nuit
- (d) une personne / avec une douche / cinq nuits

3 (a) Bonsoir mademoiselle   (b) Une chambre, s'il vous plaît
   (c) Trois personnes   (d) Avec bain (s'il vous plaît)
   (e) Quatre nuits (s'il vous plaît)   (f) (Give your own name here)

Programme numéro trois

1
six oeufs	3F20
un litre de lait	1F85
une demi-livre de beurre	5F
un kilo de bananes	3F
un kilo d'oranges	3F50
quatre tranches de jambon	6F
un paquet de biscuits	3F50
une baguette	1F10
douze petits pains	14F40
TOTAL	41F55

2 Bonjour madame / Une baguette, cinq croissants et cinq petits pains, s'il vous plaît / Lentement, s'il vous plaît / 12F10 / Merci madame, au revoir madame

3 (a) une station service   (b) la poste
   (c) une boulangerie   (d) une banque

4 Des timbres, s'il vous plaît / Grande Bretagne / Une lettre et quatre cartes postales / 5F40

5 (a) 14F20   (b) 40F50   (c) 4F60   (d) 24F40   (e) 16F55

Programme numéro quatre

1 (a) la poste   (b) le musée   (c) la poste   (d) la gare

2 (a) PASSAGE SOUTERRAIN   (b) TABAC
   (c) ÉTRANGER   (d) ACCÈS AUX QUAIS
   (e) CONSIGNE   (f) BUREAU DE CHANGE
   (g) RENSEIGNEMENTS   (h) EAU POTABLE
   (i) ATTENDEZ PIÉTONS

3   (a) 3.10 pm   (b) 6.15 pm   (c) 8.05 am
     (d) 7.59 pm   (e) 11.12 pm   (f) 6.45 am
     (g) 4.32 pm   (h) 10.25 am   (i) 11.13 am
     (j) 1.11 pm

Programme numéro cinq

1 Bonsoir mademoiselle. Une chambre, s'il vous plaît / Deux personnes / Un grand lit / Une nuit

2 (a) Deux menus à quinze francs (s'il vous plaît)
(b) Deux steaks (s'il vous plaît). Un bien cuit, avec frites et salade, et un bleu, avec salade.
(c) Un café noir et un café crème, s'il vous plaît.

3 Rouen s'il vous plaît / Aller-retour (s'il vous plaît) / Deux personnes / Oui / Lentement s'il vous plaît

4 S'il vous plaît, Monsieur, la gare? / B

5 (a) Le plein, s'il vous plaît / Super
(b) Un emplacement, s'il vous plaît
(c) douze petits pains
une demi-livre de beurre   un kilo de raisins
un demi-litre de lait   six oeufs

6 (a) D   (b) You have right of way

French–English word list

Le and *la* in front of words indicate whether they are masculine or feminine. Words which have *l'* or *les* in front of them have (m) or (f) given in brackets to show their gender.
The English meanings given here apply only to the words as they are used in this book.

A

	à	*to, at, on, in*
d'	accord	*certainly*
l'	addition (f)	*bill*
j'	ai	*I have*
	aimez-vous	*do you like?*
je n'	ai pas	*I haven't got*
	aller	*to go*
un	aller simple	*single (ticket)*
un	aller-retour	*return (ticket)*
vous	allez	*are you going? (you are going)*
	allô	*hello (telephone conversation only)*
	alors	*well then*
	anglais	*English*
l'	Angleterre (f)	*England*
l'	apéritif (m)	*aperitif*
	après	*after(wards)*
l'	argent (f)	*money*
	assez	*quite*
	au	*to/in/on/at the (with m. words)*

	au revoir	*goodbye*
	avec	*with*
vous	avez	*do you have? (you have)*
	avoir	*to have*
nous	avons	*we have*

B

la	baguette	*French bread*
le	bain	*bath*
la	banane	*banana*
la	banque	*bank*
le	beurre	*butter*
	bien	*well*
	bien cuit	*well done (meat)*
	bien sûr	*of course*
à	bientôt	*cheerio*
la	bière	*beer*
le	billet	*ticket*
	blanc	*white*
	bleu	*rare (meat)*
la	boisson	*drink*
	bonne chance!	*good luck!*
	bon voyage!	*(have a) good journey!*

	bonjour *hello*
	bonsoir *good evening*
la	boulangère *lady baker*
au	bout *at the end*
la	bouteille *bottle*
le	buffet *buffet*
le	bus *bus*
le	bureau de change *foreign exchange*

C

	ça *that*
	ça sera *that will be*
	ça va? *O.K.?*
	ça va *O.K.*
le	cabinet de toilette *separate wash basin, bidet and toilet*
le	café *coffee, café*
un	café crème *white coffee*
un	café au lait *white coffee (see page 21)*
un	café noir *black coffee*
la	carte *menu*
la	carte postale *postcard*
	ce, cet, cette *this*
	cela *that*
	cent *a hundred*
le	centime *centime*
le	centre *centre*
	c'est *it's*
	ce n'est pas *it's not*
la	chambre *room*
	changer *to change*
le	chocolat *(hot) chocolate*
	cinq *five*
	cinquante *fifty*
le	citron *lemon*
la	classe *class*
le	client *customer*
la	cliente *customer*
	combien? *how much? how many?*
	comment? *how?*
	comment allez-vous? *how are you?*
	complet *fully booked*
	compliqué *complicated*

	compris *included*
	continuer *to continue*
la	cour *courtyard*
la	crème *cream*
le	croissant *croissant*
le	croque-monsieur *toasted sandwich*

D

	dans *in*
	de *of*
	demi *half*
et	demie *half past*
	des *of the, some, any*
vous	descendez *you go down*
	descendre *to go down*
vous	désirez? *what would you like? (you'd like)*
(que)	désirez-vous? *(what) would you like?*
le	dessert *dessert*
la	destination *destination*
	deux *two*
	deuxième *second*
	différent *different*
	dire *to tell*
	direction *direction*
	dix *ten*
	dix-sept *seventeen*
	dix-huit *eighteen*
	dix-neuf *nineteen*
la	douche *shower*
	douze *twelve*
à	droite *to the right*
	(sur la/votre droite *on the/your right*)
tout	droit *straight on*
	du *some, any, of the (with m. words)*

E

l'	eau, (f) *water*
	elle *she, it*
l'	emplacement (m) *pitch on a campsite*
l'	employé (m) *clerk*
l'	employée (f) *clerk*
	en *in*
	entendu *certainly*

	environ *about*
l'	épicière *lady grocer*
l'	essence (f) *petrol*
	est-ce qu'il ya? *is there?*
l'	étage (m) *floor, storey*
	et *and*
vous	êtes *you are*

F

	facile *easy*
	faire *to do*
nous	faisons *we do*
la	femme *woman*
les	feux *traffic lights*
la	ficelle *thin French loaf*
le	flageolet *kidney bean*
le	fond *far side*
le	franc *franc*
les	frites (f) *chips*
le	fromage *cheese*
le	fruit *fruit*

G

la	gare *station*
à	gauche *to the left*
	(sur la/votre gauche *on the/your left*)
le	gramme *gramme*
	grand *large, big (double – of bed)*
la	Grande Bretagne *Great Britain*

H

	hein *eh*
l'	heure (f) *hour*
l'	homme (m) *man*
un	hot dog *a hot dog*
	huit *eight*
l'	hôtel (m) *hotel*
l'	hôtesse (f) *receptionist, assistant*
l'	huile (f) *oil*

I

d'	ici *from around here*
	il y a *there is, there are*
	il y en a un *there is one*
	important *important*
	interdit *prohibited*

J

	j'ai *I have*
le	jambon *ham*
	je *I*
le	journal *newspaper* (*plural*: journaux)
	jusqu'à *as far as*

K

le	kilo *kilo*

L

	l', la *the*
	là *there*
le	lait *milk*
au	lait *with milk*
le	le *the*
le	légume *vegetable*
	lentement *slowly*
la	lettre *letter*
le	lit *bed*
le	litre *litre*
la	livre *pound (either 500 grammes weight or £ sterling)*

M

	madame *madam, Mrs*
	mademoiselle *Miss*
	magnifique *magnificent*
	mais *but*
	maison *home-made*
la	Mairie *town hall*
	me *(to) me*
vous	me mettez *give me*
le	menu *set meal*
	merci *thank you*
	merci bien *thank you very much*
le	mètre *metre*
la	minute *minute*
	moins *to (of time)*
	moins le quart *a quarter to*
la	monnaie *currency*
	monsieur *sir, Mr.*

N

	nature *plain, nothing added*

	ne (n')... pas	*not*
	ne (n')... que	*only*
	net	*net*
	neuf	*nine*
	noir	*black*
le	nom	*name*
	non	*no*
	nous	*we*
la	nuit	*night*
le	numéro	*number*

O

l'	oeuf (m)	*egg*
	onze	*eleven*
	opposé (e)	*opposite*
l'	orange (m)	*orange*
	ordinaire	*2 star (of petrol)*
	ou	*or*
	où (est)	*where (is)*
	où y a-t-il?	*where is/ are there?*
	oui	*yes*

P

le	pain	*bread*
	pain de campagne	*cottage loaf*
le	paquet	*packet*
	par	*per*
le	parc-mètre	*parking meter*
	pardon?	*pardon*
	pardon!	*excuse me*
le	parking	*car park*
	parler	*to speak*
	pas	*not*
en	passant	*going past*
le	passeport	*passport*
le	pâté	*pâté*
la	pâtisserie	*small cake, small pastry (also cake shop)*
la	pêche melba	*peach melba*
la	personne	*person*
	petit	*small*
le	petit déjeuner	*breakfast*
le	petit pain	*soft roll*

je	peux	*can I? (I can)*
	pique-niquer	*to picnic*
la	place	*square*
	plus	*plus*
à	point	*medium (meat)*
la	pompiste	*petrol pump attendant*
la	poste	*post office*
	pour	*for*
de	préférence	*preferably*
	premier	*first*
	prendre	*to have, to take*
vous	prendrez	*you take*
	prendrez-vous?	*will you have (take)?*
vous	prenez	*you take*
	près d'ici	*near here*
	presque	*nearly*
une	pression	*a draught beer*
le	prix	*price*
	prochain	*next*

Q

	quarante	*forty*
et	quart	*quarter past (of time)*
	quatorze	*fourteen*
	quatre	*four*
	quatre-vingts	*eighty*
	quatre-vingt-dix	*ninety*
	que . . .?	*what . . .?*
	qu'est-ce que . . .?	*what . . .?*
	quel(s)	*what? or*
	quelle(s)	*which?*
	qui	*who, which*
	quinze	*fifteen*

R

les	raisins	*grapes*
le/la	réceptionniste	*receptionist*
j'ai le	regret	*I'm sorry*
	remonter	*to go back up*
j'ai	réservé	*I have booked*
le	restaurant	*restaurant*
	retourner	*return, go back*

	rosé	*rosé (wine)*
	rouge	*red*
la	route	*(main) road*
la	rue	*street, road*

S

	saignant	*medium rare (meat)*
je	sais	*I know*
la	salade	*salad*
le	sandwich	*sandwich*
le	saucisson	*a type of salami*
	second(e)	*second*
	seize	*sixteen*
le	self service (le self)	*self-service restaurant*
	sept	*seven*
la	serveuse	*waitress*
le	service	*service*
vous	signez	*will you sign? (you sign)*
	s'il vous plaît!!	*to attract someone's attention*
	s'il vous plaît	*please*
	simple	*easy*
	six	*six*
le	soir	*evening*
	soixante	*sixty*
	soixante-dix	*seventy*
	soixante et un	*sixty one*
nous	sommes	*we are*
la	soupe	*soup*
le	steak	*steak*
je	suis	*I am*
	super	*4-star (of petrol)*
	sur	*on*
le	Syndicat d'Initiative	*tourist office*

T

la	taxe	*tax*
le	thé	*tea*
	thé au lait	*tea with milk*
	thé citron	*tea with lemon*
	thé nature	*tea with nothing added*
le	timbre	*stamp*

les	toilettes	*toilets*
le	touriste	*tourist*
	touristique	*tourist*
	tourner	*to turn*
vous	tournez	*you turn*
	tout de suite	*immediately*
	tout	*all*
	tout droit	*straight on*
de	toute manière	*anyway*
le	train	*train*
la	tranche	*slice*
le	traveller's (check)	*traveller's cheque*
	très	*very*
	très bien	*very well*
	treize	*thirteen*
	trente	*thirty*
	trois	*three*
	troisième	*third*
	trouver	*to find*

U

	un(e)	*a, one*

V

je	vais	*I'm going*
il	vaut mieux que	*you'd be better*
la	vendeuse	*assistant*
vous	venez	*you are coming*
la	viande	*meat*
la	ville	*town*
le	vin	*wine*
	vingt	*twenty*
	vingt et un	*twenty one*
	voici	*here (is/are)*
	voilà	*there!*
	voir	*to see*
	votre/vos	*your*
je	voudrais	*I'd like*
vous	voulez	*do you want? (you want)*
	vous	*you*
le	voyageur	*traveller*

Z

	zéro	*zero*

English–French word list

A
a *un(e)*
about *environ*
after(wards) *après*
a hundred *cent*
all *tout*
and *et*
anyway *de toute manière*
aperitif *l'apéritif (m)*
a quarter to *moins le quart*
(we) are *nous sommes*
as far as *jusqu'à*
assistant *la vendeuse*
at *à*
at the (with masculine words) *au*
at the end of *au bout de*
at (to) your right (left) *à votre droite (gauche)*
attendant (at petrol pump) *la pompiste*

B
baker *la boulangère*
banana *la banane*
bank *la banque*
bath *le bain*
bed *le lit*
beer *la bière*
  draught beer *une pression*
better *mieux*
  you'd be better *il vaut mieux que*
bill *l'addition (f)*
biscuit *le biscuit*
black *noir*
to book (reserve) *réserver*
  I have booked *j'ai réservé*
bottle *la bouteille*
bread *le pain*
  cottage loaf *le pain de campagne*
  French style bread *la baguette*
  thin French loaf *la ficelle*

breakfast *le petit déjeuner*
buffet *le buffet*
bus *le bus*
but *mais*
butcher's *la boucherie*
butter *le beurre*

C
cake shop *la pâtisserie*
cafe *le café*
can I? *je peux?*
car park *le parking*
centime *le centime*
centre *le centre*
certainly *d'accord; entendu*
(to) change *changer*
cheerio *à bientôt*
cheese *le fromage*
cheese store *la fromagerie*
chips *les frites (f)*
chocolate *le chocolat*
cider *le cidre*
class *la classe*
clerk *l'employé(e) (m)(f)*
coffee *le café*
  black *le café noir*
  with cream *café crème*
  with hot milk *café au lait*
complicated *compliqué*
(to) continue *continuer*
courtyard *la cour*
cream *la crème*
croissant *le croissant*
currency *la monnaie*

D
dairy produce *la laiterie*
dessert *le dessert*
destination *la destination*
different *différent*
direction *la direction*
(to) do *faire*
  we do *nous faisons*
double bed *le lit grand*

draught beer *une pression*
drink *la boisson*

E

easy *facil; simple*
egg *l'oeuf (m)*
eh *hein*
eight *huit*
eighty *quatre-vingts*
eleven *onze*
end *le bout*
  at the end of *au bout de*
England *l'Angleterre (f)*
English *l'anglais (m)*
evening *le soir*
  good evening *bonsoir*
excuse me! *pardon!*

F

far side *le fond*
fifteen *quinze*
fifty *cinquante*
(to) find *trouver*
five *cinq*
floor (story) *l'étage (f)*
for *pour*
foreign exchange *le bureau de change*
forty *quarante*
four *quatre*
fourteen *quatorze*
franc *le franc*
fruit *le fruit*
fully booked *complet*

G

give me (during a purchase) *vous me mettez*
(to) go *aller*
  (are you) going? (you are going) *vous allez*
  (I'm) going *je vais*
(to) go back *retourner*
(to) go back up *remonter*
(to) go down *descendre*
  (you) go down *vous descendez*
goodbye *au revoir*
good evening *bonsoir*

(have a) good journey *bon voyage!*
good luck! *bonne chance!*
gramme *le gramme*
Great Britain *la Grande Bretagne*
grocer *l'épicière (f)*
grocer's *l'épicerie; l'alimentation (f)*
grapes *les raisins (m)*

H

half *demi*
half past . . . *et demie*
ham *le jambon*
have a good journey! *bon voyage!*
have you? *vous avez?; avez-vous?*
  I have *j'ai*
  I haven't got (don't have) *je n'ai pas*
  we have *nous avons*
(to) have (take) *prendre*
  will you have (take) *prendrez-vous?*
  you take *vous prenez*
hello *allô (telephone); bonjour*
here is (are) *voici*
home-made *maison*
hostess (receptionist, assistant) *l'hôtesse (f)*
a hot dog *un hot dog*
hotel *l'hôtel*
hour *l'heure (f)*
how are you? *comment allez-vous?*
how many?; how much? *combien?*
(a) hundred *cent*

I

I *je*
I am *je suis*
I am going *je vais*
I am sorry *j'ai le regret*
I have *j'ai*
I know *je sais*

I would like *je voudrais*
ice cream *la glace*
immediately *tout de suite*
important *important(e)*
in *dans; en; à*
included *compris*
is there? *est-ce qu'il y a?*
it (f) *elle*
it's *c'est*
it's not *ce n'est pas*

J

jam *la confiture*
journey *le voyage*
  have a good journey! *bon voyage!*
juice *le jus*

K

kidney bean *le flageolet*
kilogram *le kilo*

L

large *grand(e)*
(to, on the) left *à (sur la) gauche*
lemon *le citron*
letter *la lettre*
(do you) like? *aimez-vous?*
(I'd) like *je voudrais*
litre *le litre*

M

magnificent *magnifique*
man *l'homme (m)*
meat *la viande*
medium rare *saignant*
medium well *à point*
menu *la carte*
meter *le mètre*
milk *le lait*
  with milk *au lait*
minute *la minute*
Miss *mademoiselle*
Mr; sir *monsieur*
Mrs; madam *madame*
money *l'argent (m)*

N

name *le nom*
near here *près d'ici*
nearly *presque*
net *net*
newspaper *le journal*
next *prochain(e)*
night *la nuit*
nine *neuf*
ninety *quatre-vingt-dix*
no *non*
nothing added *(to a drink or food) nature*
number *le numéro*

O

occupied *occupé(e)*
of *de*
  of the *du; des*
of course *bien sûr*
O.K. *ça va*
oil *l'huile (f)*
on *sur*
one *un(e)*
only *ne . . . que*
opposite *opposé(e)*
or *ou*
orange *l'orange (m)*

P

package *le paquet*
pancake *la crêpe*
pancake shop *crêperie*
pardon! *pardon!*
parking meter *le parcmètre*
(going) past *en passant*
passport *le passeport*
pastry shop *la pâtisserie*
paté *le paté*
peach melba *la pêche melba*
per *par*
person *la personne*
petrol *l'essence (f)*
  two-star petrol *ordinaire*
  four-star petrol *super*
petrol pump attendant *la pompiste*
to picnic *pique-niquer*
pitch (on a campsite) *l'emplacement (m)*

plain *nature*
please *s'il vous plaît*
plus *plus*
post office *la poste*
postcard *la carte postale*
pound *la livre*
preferable *de préférence*
price *le prix*
printed matter *imprimés*
prohibited *interdit*

Q
(a) quarter to . . . *moins le quart*
(a) quarter past . . . *et quart*
quite *assez*

R
rare (meat) *bleu*
  medium rare *saignant*
receptionist *l'hôtesse (f); le, la receptionniste*
red *rouge*
restaurant *le restaurant*
(to) return *retourner*
(to, on the) right *à (sur la) droite*
road *la route*
roll *le petit pain*
room *la chambre*
rosé (wine) *rosé*

S
salad *la salade*
salami (sausage) *le saucisson*
sandwich *le sandwich*
second *second(e); deuxième*
(to) see *voir*
self service *le self service; le self*
service *le service*
set meal *le menu*
seven *sept*
seventeen *dix-sept*
seventy *soixante-dix*
she *elle*
shower *la douche*

(to) sign *signer*
  will you sign? *vous signez?; signez-vous?*
sir *Monsieur*
six *six*
sixty *soixante*
sixty-one *soixante et un*
slice *la tranche*
slowly *lentement*
small *petit(e)*
small cake *la pâtisserie*
small pastry *la pâtisserie*
some *des; du; quelques*
soup *la soupe*
(to) speak *parler*
square *la place*
stamp *le timbre*
station *la gare*
steak *le steak*
story *l'étage (f)*
straight on *tout droit*
street *la rue*

T
tax *le taxe*
tea *le thé*
  plain tea *thé nature*
  with lemon *thé citron*
  with milk *thé au lait*
(to) tell *dire*
ten *dix*
thank you (very much) *merci (bien; beaucoup)*
that *ça; cela*
that will be *ça sera*
the *l', la, le, les*
there *là; y*
there! *voilà!*
there is *il y a*
third *troisième*
thirteen *treize*
thirty *trente*
three *trois*
this *ce; cet; cette*
ticket *le billet*
  one-way *un aller simple*
  round-trip *un aller retour*
toasted sandwich *le croque-monsieur*

toilet *la toilette; les toilettes*
  with bidet, wash basin, and
  stool *le cabinet de*
  toilette
tourist *le touriste; touristique*
tourist office *le Syndicat*
  d'Initiative
town *la ville*
Town (City) Hall *la Mairie*
traffic lights *les feux*
train *le train*
traveller *le voyageur*
traveller's check *le*
  traveller's
(to) turn *tourner*
  you turn *vous tournez*
twelve *douze*
twenty *vingt*
twenty-one *vingt et un*
two *deux*
two-star (petrol) *ordinaire*

V
vacant *libre*
vegetable *le légume*
very well *très bien*

W
waitress *la serveuse*
(to) want *vouloir*
  do you want? *voulez-vous?*

water *l'eau (f)*
we *nous*
well *bien*
well done *bien cuit*
well then *alors*
what? *que?*
what do you want?; what
  would you like? *qu'est-ce*
  que vous voulez?; que
  voulez (désirez) vous?
where is? *où est?; où y a-t-il?*
which *qui*
white *blanc (blanche)*
who *qui*
will you take (have)? *prendrez-*
  vous?
wine *le vin*
with milk *au lait*

Y
yes *oui*
you *vous*
you are *vous êtes*
your *votre, vos*

Z
zero *zéro*

ITINERARY

DATE	PLACE

ITINERARY

DATE	PLACE

ITINERARY

DATE	PLACE

EXPENSES			
DATE	AMT.	U.S.$	FOR:

EXPENSES			
DATE	AMT.	U.S.$	FOR:

EXPENSES			
DATE	AMT.	U.S.$	FOR:

EXPENSES			
DATE	AMT.	U.S.$	FOR:

EXPENSES			
DATE	AMT.	U.S.$	FOR:

EXPENSES			
DATE	AMT.	U.S.$	FOR:

EXPENSES			
DATE	AMT.	U.S.$	FOR:

EXPENSES			
DATE	AMT.	U.S.$	FOR:

PURCHASES

ITEM _____

WHERE BOUGHT _____

GIFT FOR _____COST_____U.S.$_____

ITEM _____

WHERE BOUGHT _____

GIFT FOR _____COST_____U.S.$_____

ITEM _____

WHERE BOUGHT _____

GIFT FOR _____COST_____U.S.$_____

ITEM _____

WHERE BOUGHT _____

GIFT FOR _____COST_____U.S.$_____

ITEM _____

WHERE BOUGHT _____

GIFT FOR _____COST_____U.S.$_____

PURCHASES

ITEM _____

WHERE BOUGHT _____

GIFT FOR _____ COST _____ U.S.$ _____

ITEM _____

WHERE BOUGHT _____

GIFT FOR _____ COST _____ U.S.$ _____

ITEM _____

WHERE BOUGHT _____

GIFT FOR _____ COST _____ U.S.$ _____

ITEM _____

WHERE BOUGHT _____

GIFT FOR _____ COST _____ U.S.$ _____

ITEM _____

WHERE BOUGHT _____

GIFT FOR _____ COST _____ U.S.$ _____

PURCHASES

ITEM _____

WHERE BOUGHT _____

GIFT FOR _____COST_____U.S.$_____

ITEM _____

WHERE BOUGHT _____

GIFT FOR _____ COST_____U.S.$_____

ITEM _____

WHERE BOUGHT _____

GIFT FOR _____COST_____U.S.$_____

ITEM _____

WHERE BOUGHT _____

GIFT FOR _____ COST_____U.S.$_____

ITEM _____

WHERE BOUGHT _____

GIFT FOR _____ COST_____U.S.$_____

ADDRESSES

NAME _____

ADDRESS _____

_____ PHONE _____

NAME _____

ADDRESS _____

_____ PHONE _____

NAME _____

ADDRESS _____

_____ PHONE _____

NAME _____

ADDRESS _____

_____ PHONE _____

NAME _____

ADDRESS _____

_____ PHONE _____

ADDRESSES

NAME _____

ADDRESS _____

_____ PHONE_____

NAME _____

ADDRESS _____

_____ PHONE_____

NAME _____

ADDRESS _____

_____ PHONE_____

NAME _____

ADDRESS _____

_____ PHONE_____

NAME _____

ADDRESS _____

_____ PHONE_____

ADDRESSES

NAME _____

ADDRESS _____

_____ PHONE _____

NAME _____

ADDRESS _____

_____ PHONE _____

NAME _____

ADDRESS _____

_____ PHONE _____

NAME _____

ADDRESS _____

_____ PHONE _____

NAME _____

ADDRESS _____

_____ PHONE _____

TRAVEL DIARY

DATE_____

DATE_____

DATE_____

DATE_____

DATE_____

DATE_____

DATE_____

TRAVEL DIARY

DATE_____

DATE_____

DATE_____

DATE_____

DATE_____

DATE_____

DATE_____

TRAVEL DIARY

DATE_____

DATE_____

DATE_____

DATE_____

DATE_____

DATE_____

DATE_____

TRAVEL DIARY

DATE_____

DATE_____

DATE_____

DATE_____

DATE_____

DATE_____

DATE_____

TRAVEL DIARY

DATE_____

DATE_____

DATE_____

DATE_____

DATE_____

DATE_____

DATE_____

TRAVEL DIARY

DATE_____

DATE_____

DATE_____

DATE_____

DATE_____

DATE_____

DATE_____